Let the Spirit Breathe

Personal Psalms, Prayers, and Pieces

By Danny A. Belrose

Herald Publishing House
Independence, Missouri

Copyright © 2004
Herald Publishing House
Independence, Missouri
All rights reserved.
Illustrations by Amber Mills

Produced and distributed by:

Herald Publishing House
1001 W. Walnut
P.O. Box 390
Independence, MO 64051-0390
Phone: 1-800-767-8181 or (816) 521-3015
Fax: (816) 521-3066
Web site: *www.HeraldHouse.org*

Printed in the United States of America
ISBN 0-8309-1130-8

Library of Congress Cataloging-in-Publication Data

Belrose, Danny A., 1941-
Let the spirit breathe : personal psalms, prayers, and pieces / by Danny A. Belrose.-- 1st ed.
    p. cm.
Includes bibliographical references.
ISBN 0-8309-1130-8
1. Prayer--Christianity. 2. Prayers. I. Title.
BV210.3.B45 2004
242--dc22

2004018796

Contents

Preface

Tell me what prayer is, will you?
Head bowed, *sometimes*; fingers laced, *sometimes*;
Eyes closed, *sometimes*; deep sighs, *sometimes*;
Heavy on the compliments and praise *always*!
   "Nice job putting things together, God; very creative!"
   "Great food! Thanks for my family, my job, my retirement plan."
A good word or two for sunshine, blue skies, and 1 percent milk,
And the beat goes on in care of *God24/7@gol.com.*

Cyberspace-spam prayers filling up heaven's hardrive,
wrapped up in shopping lists of needs and wants,
tagged affectionately with *"Your will be done,*
but lean things my way if you can" aspirations.

It's *more* than that, of course.
It's unplugging yourself from center stage.
It's taking time out and time in.
It's hearing your own heartbeat,
      feeling air on the palms of your hands,
      remembering there are feet inside your shoes,
      seeing a constellation in a tea cup,
      discovering the universe on a blade of grass,
      catching color that has no name, at sunset.

It's a minute or two of *breathing lessons*
      —the awareness you are alive, thank God!
Because so often, we are not.

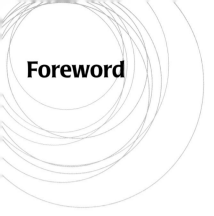

Foreword

Where is God when it's raining?
Why is God sometimes on vacation?
Is God "out there"—deep within us—"none of the above" or both?
What is prayer and who is listening?
Is praying a waste of time—or is time a waste of prayer?
Does the Spirit breathe in me and through me?
Is God ever short of breath?

It's a matter of routine. She calculates fat grams, counts carbs, and does twenty on the treadmill. Orange juice. Eyeliner. Lipstick. She grabs a low-cal snack for a lunch meeting, reschedules a hair appointment, drops off the kids, and heads for the office. She's out of breath when she gets there. Out of breath when she leaves. Scrambled dinner with the family, kitchen clean-up, twenty minutes with a novel, and an hour of TV. Checks for utilities and MasterCard™, the late-night news, some catch-up conversation in the quiet of night with the man she loves beside her, and finally . . . *silence*. Silence and the sound of shallow breathing in search of sleep. *Where has the week gone?* It's a matter of routine. Tomorrows are reruns, and God breathes for one hour each Sunday.

In *The Ruling Class*, actor Peter O'Toole portrays the fourteenth Earl of Gurney, "a paranoid schizophrenic," who thinks he is God. When asked how he *knows* he is God, he replies, "Simple. When I pray to Him, I find I'm talking to myself."

Sound familiar? This is a book for people who talk to themselves and talk to God—and who *sometimes* cannot distinguish between self-talk and God-talk. It is a book for people who need "breathing lessons"—who need the Spirit to breathe *on* them, *in* them, and *through* them. It's about expanding God's shortness of breath in us. It's about giving God room in the helter-skelter of everydayness where life's vibrant spirit is frequently squelched and short-lived. This is a book about *letting the Spirit breathe.*

This is not a "how to" manual or a "what if" theological treatise. It does not unfold deep mysteries of the universe, cast a blinding light of relief on the dark night of the soul, nor delve into hidden secrets of meditation. It is a collection of stream of consciousness writings, reflections, and personal psalms that express my ongoing journey for self-identity, spiritual connection, and renewal.

An old proverb says, "God comes to us without a bell." In other words, God's renewal is promised, but it comes silently, unseen, without fanfare, but in many different ways. God's Spirit has chased me and found me in subtle and unexpected ways while spilling thoughts onto a computer monitor as I have taken time to waste time—unstructured time with God *inside* and *out*.

In our busy, demanding, hi-tech world it seems increasingly difficult to "make way" or to find time for God. We gulp life instead of savoring it, intent on filling every moment rather than having moments fill us. "Time is too valuable to waste!" has become our litany. I am not immune to this dictum. I have to discipline myself to *waste time with God, to allow the enlivening Spirit of God to breathe in me anew*—and yet when I do—renewal comes surely and wonderfully.

What is in this collection for you? Some ponderings and questions, a turn of a phrase, an occasional lover's quarrel with faith, and a connection with a spiritual journey not unlike your own. In short—I trust it will provide grist for your spiritual mill and entice you to take time for self-talk and God-talk. Hopefully you will find herein that which will spur your own spiritual journey and encourage you to "let the Spirit breathe."

"Listen carefully to your own journey as a people,
for it is a sacred journey yet to come . . .
Let the Spirit breathe."

—W. Grant McMurray

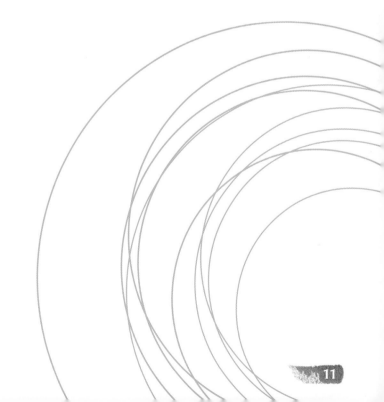

Wasting Time with God:
Inviting the Spirit to Breathe

If prayers were dollars, I'd be bankrupt!
Oh, I know, now and then
    I go online and slip in a few praises,
    a couple of thank-yous, and a shopping list.
But shouldn't prayer be more than that?
A cool drink of water. A splash of sunset.
A dog's bark. A violin solo.

If prayer were seeing the color of morning,
    tasting the salt air of seaside,
    or feeling the bite of winter wind,
    I'd still be bankrupt.
It's happening all around me
    and I fail to drink it in.

Sipping life isn't prayer unless you taste it.
Let me roll it around on my tongue a little.
I really must turn the light on
    and see what's there.
I think if I could, that *would* be prayer!

"Take a deep breath and hold it," says the doctor pressing an ice-cold stethoscope to your quivering chest. *Pneuma,* the Greek word in the New Testament translated as "spirit," also refers to breath or breeze. Likewise, the Hebrew *nshameh* means not only "spirit" but "wind, angry or vital breath, and divine inspiration." God is closer than breath itself. Take a deep breath and hold it! Breathe in deeply God's goodness and grace and hold them in awhile—lest they escape our notice and thanksgiving. Then breathe them out as God's blessing.

This is a book of prayers, reflections, and hymns composed while *wasting time with God*—times when I slowed down long enough to let the Spirit breathe on me, in me, and through me. Although they voice my spiritual journey, I hope you will hear—in and between the lines—your own voice. With the help of such notables as Henri Nouwen and Anthony Bloom, I have placed these offerings within the following metaphors of prayer:

- Prayer as Death and Resurrection
- Prayer as Positive Disillusionment
- Prayer as Unemployed Worker
- Prayer as Positive Selfishness
- Prayer as Passive Voice
- Prayer as Hospitable Host

"Wasting time with God" (a phrase borrowed from Nouwen) begs further clarification. My intention in using it is to widen the embrace of prayer beyond conventional ritualization. Joseph Campbell said, "All of life is meditation, most of it unintentional." Luke suggests that prayer should be unceasing, "Watch ye therefore, and pray always" (21:35, King James version). The New Revised Standard Version softens this mandate to "Be alert at all times, praying"—while Eugene H. Peterson's *The Message: The Bible in Contemporary Language* says, "Pray constantly that you will have the strength and wits to make it through everything that's coming and end up on your feet before the Son of Man."[1] I like that. Prayer should help us end up on our feet. But how does one pray unceasingly? Obviously one cannot go through life with head bowed and eyes tightly closed.

Easton's Bible Dictionary defines prayer as "'beseeching the Lord' (Exodus 32:11); 'pouring out the soul before the Lord' (I Samuel 1:15); 'praying and crying to heaven' (II Chronicles 32:20); 'seeking unto God and making supplication' (Job 8:5); 'bowing the knees' (Ephesians 3:14); 'drawing near to God' (Psalm 73:28)." [2]

Any time we draw near to God we are in praye[r]... [lan]guage of spirituality—and spirituality is paying attention to life. It is having a lively awareness of our relationship with self, others, the created order, and its Author. Prayer then is both act and attitude—spoken and unspoken. It finds its voice on bowed knee or leather armchair. It can tumble into the mind and out of the soul during a stroll in the rain or backpacking through the mountains. It can claim us in the sanctuary, the subway, or the solitude of the beach. It is an act of grace. It is something we do and something we are.

Yet prayer is not everything and anything. All emphasis is no emphasis. A circle without a circumference embraces nothing. Acts and attitudes that deaden us to life, that separate us from "drawing near" to God, are not prayer. Prayer ties us back to God.

Alfred North Whitehead once said, "Religion is what one does with his or her solitariness." The word religion comes from the Latin *religare* meaning *to restrain—to tie back.* The personal psalms and reflections in the pages that follow are "tie-backs." They emerged from moments of solitude, contemplation, and (frequently) spiritual agitation—moments of structured and unstructured *emptiness* with God. These were not "Oh, let's-write-a-prayer" exercises. Sometimes they were sacred silences— pregnant pauses—simply sitting smack dab in the midst of life, desperately trying to block out all the competing voices that constantly claim my attention. Doing nothing with God and being OK with that. Thinking and not thinking. Writing and not writing. Just *being.* I recommend such sacred slothfulness—it's often food for the soul.

Waste some time with this book. It is not intended to be read cover to cover. Its contents were not initially written for publication; they voice my personal journey, my own breathing lessons with God. As you enter its pages listen to your own voice, *your* questions—*your* spiritual beefs and bouquets. Get in touch with *your* path of discipleship. Take time for silence. Jot down thoughts and ideas. Write some of your own psalms. Don't rush the process. Let it happen in its own time. Let it become as natural as breathing in and breathing out. Focused and unfocused. Take some deep breaths with God and allow the Spirit rhythm. You will be surprised at what God has to say *inside* and *out.*

Part 1 | Breathing Lessons

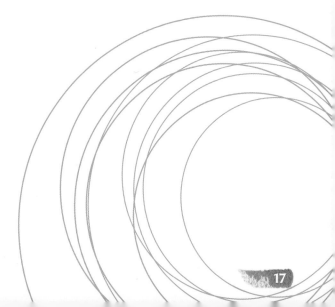

*I looked, . . . but there was no breath in them. Then he said to
me, "Prophesy to the breath, prophesy, mortal, and say to the
breath: Thus says the Lord GOD: Come from the four winds,
O breath, and breathe upon these slain, that they may live."
I prophesied as he commanded me, and the breath came into
them, and they lived, and stood on their feet, a vast multitude.*
—Ezekiel 37:8–10 NRSV

"Prophesy to the *breath*?" What a strange phrase. How does one
prophesy to *breath*? Breath in this text is the Hebrew word *rucha*, which
means (among other things) "spirit, mind, heart, the divine power of
God." Prophecy or divine utterance is not centered in foretelling but *forth
telling*. God's word empowers life. Isaiah said God's word will not return
empty (Isaiah 55:11); it creates the potential it speaks. Between the lines
of this passage I hear God saying, "Speak my word boldly, Ezekiel. By the
power of my Spirit speak forth the truth that I am the giver and restorer of
life. For *my* breath (my spirit, my mind, my heart, my power)—*is* life!"

Ezekiel's valley of dry bones is not exclusive real estate. It makes
room for everyone. I've taken up residence there from time to time when
"there was no breath" (God's breath) in me. Times when I've existed
but not been *alive*. There is a vast difference between existing and being
fully alive. The glory of God is men and women, and boys and girls, *fully
alive*! When we just exist we're like "*the walking dead*"—people who
have dry bones, dry spirits, dry attitudes, and dry hopes. We need God's
"wave offering" of new life—-we need "breathing lessons."

Pentecost: God's Breath of New Life!

Come, Holy Spirit, come. Come, Holy Spirit, come.
As we lift this invitation—rest upon this congregation.
Come, Holy Spirit, come.[3]

And come it did! With wind and fire and tongues and bread and baptisms! The Holy Spirit certainly came in dramatic fashion on Pentecost!

The Hebrew Bible celebrates Pentecost as a "holy convocation," a day on which no servile work was to be done. Male attendance was mandatory at the three principal feasts: Passover, Pentecost, and Tabernacles:

> Three times a year all your males shall appear before the LORD your God at the place that he will choose: at the festival of unleavened bread, at the festival of weeks, and at the festival of booths [or tabernacles; Hebrew *succoth*]. They shall not appear before the LORD empty-handed.
> —Deuteronomy 16:16 NRSV

Pentecost means "fiftieth." In the Hebrew Bible it was the "Feast of Weeks"—seven weeks plus one day following Passover and signaling its conclusion. Sometimes Pentecost was referred to as the Feast of Harvest or Day of the First fruits. It was a day of thanksgiving and celebration. Two loaves of leavened bread baked with the flour from the new grain harvest were presented as "wave offerings" [see KJV, Leviticus 23:15; called "elevation offerings," NRSV].

Countless sermons have been preached about Pentecost and its "breathing lessons." Breathing lessons? Yes, let's set aside the fire, the tongues, the sermon, the bread, and baptisms, and say something about the "wind," "spirit," and "breath." (The Greek word *pneuma* is used for all these terms.) The ancients frequently correlated the wind with God. After all, wind is invisible. It comes from nowhere and goes where it wills, and its effects can be mild or mighty. Thus, the God of wind and breathing!

In the intertestamental period and later, Pentecost was regarded as the anniversary of the law-giving at Sinai—a celebration of God *breathing* the life of law and discipline into God's people. But let's move the calendar ahead to Acts chapter 2. Here's Peter. It's Pentecost. It's approximately nine o'clock in the morning. Luke's account does not specify that Peter and the disciples have fulfilled their obligatory appearance at a synagogue or the temple. Perhaps they arrived before the rush and got home in time for breakfast. Nevertheless, they are about to experience a new "wave offering." God is about to breathe again in a rather profound and spectacular way: the wind, the fire, the tongues, the bread, and baptisms. God breathes and the old becomes new! Suddenly, they are experiencing a *holy convocation*, the breathing of God's Spirit (certainly not for the first time on these followers) but with "*the sound like a blowing of a violent wind...from heaven*"—and Pentecost takes on new meaning!

Pentecost will now be celebrated as the birth of Christ's community. Pentecost will now serve as a memorial and celebration of God breathing a spirit of blessing upon the church—a "wave offering," so to speak; a call and response: *backward* in memory of the firstfruits of Jesus, *forward* in terms of the call for each of us to bear the fruits of the Spirit in our lives. Law, love, spirit, and response in equal partnership. A generous God—a generous response.

Thus, Pentecost is more than a feast day; it is an act and an attitude. We should be pentecostal! I am not talking about tent meetings, altar calls, and charismatic, pulpit-pounding preachers. I am talking about servant-leaders who help people experience the fresh breath of God in their lives. We are pentecostal when we live out our Christian commitment as spiritual companions, teacher-learners, and apostolic witnesses. We are pentecostal when we provide a ministry of sanctuary—a pastoral presence of safety, acceptance, and counsel to those tossed to and fro by life's storms. We are pentecostal when we offer prayers of blessing, formal and informal. It's a matter of giving *breathing lessons*. And breathing lessons begin at home. They begin with an honest assessment of God's breath in our own lives.

In his autobiography, *Here I Stand*, Episcopal bishop John Shelby Spong shares a significant "breathing lesson" concerning prayer. He visited a young wife and mother dying from terminal cancer who opened her life to him. She shared honestly and deeply about her fears, hopes, disappointments, and questions. Bishop Spong was deeply moved by her trust and the privilege she extended to him in seeing into her life. However, he found his ministerial response wanting:

> When the time came for me to leave, not knowing quite what to say, I asked if I could pray with her. That was, I am sure, something I felt was a role expectation. She did not object, so holding her hand in mine, I said a prayer. I do not recall the words of that prayer, but I will never forget my feelings about it. It was phony and pious God-talk, made up of one religious cliché after another. I was embarrassed about it when it was over. It added nothing to the depth of our conversation or to the meaning of our relationship. Indeed, if anything, it detracted from both. I thanked her for the time we had shared and promised to visit her at least once a week while she was in Charlottesville.
>
> On the drive home I kept coming back to the contrast between the reality present in the conversation and the lack of reality present in the words of the prayer. The former expanded both of our lives. The latter contracted at least my life and, I suspected, hers as well. If prayer contracted life, I wondered, was it still prayer? If conversation that was deep and genuine expanded life, then was that conversation not a prayer? I wondered if I had my designations wrong. If I could not pray with honesty then, I asked myself, could I really pray at all? I have never had a more critical conversation with myself, and the issue would not simply go away. I vowed I would never again pray in a pastoral visit until I could pray with as much honesty as I could find in my ability to talk with and to the person I was visiting.[4]

Spong experienced his own Pentecost—*a holy convocation*—a stirring of God's breath that was disturbing and transforming. We would do well to consistently seek such convocation in our ministry, our lives, and our most private devotions.

Wind, fire, tongues, bread, and baptisms—Pentecost! Can we feel God's breath rushing in? Or does the breeze pass us by? Breathing is an involuntary action—so automatic, so natural it escapes notice only when we are out of breath, when we desperately claw to the surface of a wave, gasping for air, and take God in. That's what breathing is, you know. It's *taking God in*, because *GOD IS LIFE!* And that's what worship is. Worship is singing hymns, preaching sermons, saying prayers. Worship is holy silence, meditation, and reflection. It's *taking God in* whether we be in sanctuary or solitude. Worship can be that brief pause at the computer keyboard when your gaze catches the blur of bird's wing at the window. It can be a line from a song slipping into your mind, the color of sunset that takes your breath away and gives it back again renewed. Worship can be anytime, anywhere, when life and love break in and the old becomes new. And worship in *all* its forms is a Pentecost—a "*holy convocation*"—a breathing lesson!

Come then, Holy Spirit, breathe on us
  —fill us with life anew!
Grace us with new depths of honesty, integrity, and sensitivity.
Grant us new eyes to see the hidden gifts of friend, family, and stranger.
Open unfettered highways of trust, appreciation, and
  transforming friendship.
Let leadership and management be eclipsed by ministry.
Let not public performance impoverish personal piety.
And finally, gracious God, stir within us the true spirit of servanthood
  —remind us of why we do what we do
  —the call, the passion, the joy, the hope, the tears, the great laughter.
Give us breathing lessons!
Breathe on us that we may stir your breath of life in others!
In Jesus name we pray. Amen.

One Fervent Prayer

"Let us breathe one fervent prayer, Ere from hence our footsteps tend."[5]
*So goes the hymn, God. The hope to breathe one fervent prayer–the hope to sense the
sweet breeze of your presence in our midst. Hear then our plea . . .*

Let the breath of your Spirit stir our souls with new resolve
> to be your sons and daughters.
Let it sweep from our lives lost days, dusty dreams, leftover love.
Let the breath of your Spirit come gently–refreshing our insights for your
> church and people.
Let it waft new hope and assurance into hearts made heavy
> by unrest and uncertainty.
Let it enlighten and encourage your servants–
> blessing them with courage, strength, and a lightness of spirit.
> And when worry and weariness invade–grace them
>> with solitude and retreat,
> breathing your renewal upon them.

May the breath of your Spirit come also, dear God, as a *mighty wind*–
Let it roll the stones away–
> the stones we place at the sepulcher of our private lives
> where even they, whom we cherish most, have no admittance.
Let it roll away the stones we lay between sisters and brothers of the faith
> who behave and believe differently–
> whose God seems so distant from ours.
Let it roll away the stones we pretend are not there–
> stones that separate colleagues, quorums, and councils–
> stones that replace fellowship with policy, and care with convenience.
Let it break down our defenses–releasing the stale air of self-sufficiency
> that we might lean again upon your arms.

Part 2

Letting the Spirit Breathe
at the Edges of Life:
Prayer as Death and Resurrection

People say that what we're all seeking is a meaning for life. I don't think that's what we're really seeking. I think that what we're seeking is an experience of being alive, so that our life experiences on the purely physical plane will have resonances within our own innermost being and reality, so that we actually feel the rapture of being alive.[6]—Joseph Campbell

It's been said that the tragedy of life is not in the fact of death, but what dies inside people while they still live—the death of genuine feeling, the death of inspired response. Ironically, the opposite is also tragic. It is what lives inside a person that prevents death from claiming that which should die in order for new life to be. Self-sufficiency, self-centeredness, pride, overt materialism, and aggrandizement—idolatry in all its many disguises—are but a few of the many "lively" characteristics that should be put to death. In metaphorical language, prayer is both death and resurrection. Prayer can serve as cross, burial ground, and empty tomb for negative propensities that are inhibiting and destructive.

Prayer as cross confronts us with the fact that we are "malefactors." Isaiah cried out, "Woe is me! I am lost, for I am a man of unclean lips, and I live among a people of unclean lips; yet my eyes have seen the King, the Lord of hosts!" (Isaiah 6:5 NRSV). Isaiah experienced his presence with and at the same time his absence from God.

We cannot acknowledge our presence before God without sensing our chosen alienation from God. Sin is alienation and separation rooted

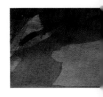

in selfishness; it is refusal of our creaturehood. The awareness of God's presence reveals to us that we have tended to position ourselves where God rightly belongs—at the moral center of our lives. We recognize we are not where we should be; we are not who we should be.

It is the contrite heart then, not God, that determines prayer's venue as cross. God does not drive in the nails. Welcomed and accepted by God, we, nevertheless, experience the contrast between God and self and the void separating who we are from who we could be. We judge ourselves and find ourselves wanting.

Prayer as empty tomb promises new beginnings. Before the raising of Lazarus, the embarrassed Martha cautioned Jesus not to disturb the tomb: ". . . there is a stench because he has been dead four days" (John 11:39 NRSV). The same stone that keeps decay and foul air trapped inside prevents the entrance of fresh air. Prayer as empty tomb is open tomb. It provides the setting where refreshment and resurrection begin. It allows us to deal openly and honestly with angst, quandaries, and uncertainties. It gives us permission to vent and to lament—to argue with one's God, one's faith, and one's self—in a safe place where stones have been rolled away.

Prayer as empty tomb resurrects us to new priorities and possibilities. It is coming alive to a new self, coming alive to "significant others," and alive to others who are *suddenly* more significant. It is coming alive to the gift of life (Campbell's "rapture of feeling alive") wherein we seize each waking moment with thanksgiving.

Time

I'm thinking about *time,* God.
Past and future—dying and birthing within a constant now.
Time, a precious gift constantly slipping away—enfolding our fleeting edges
 of mortality, pressing us to make the most of that which is.
Sweep-second hands whisper,
 "Tomorrow holds no promise, drink deeply now;
 the grains of sand slip quickly!"
Time—a gift you never need, God.
Unfettered by its ticking walls
 —you have not been nor *will be* but *ARE.*

What *is* time? A measurement of events?
A sequence of happenings?
A continuum of space, light, gravity?
Is it linear? Can it be bent, folded, revisited?
How difficult to define, how demanding, how unforgiving!
A split second and lives are irrevocably changed.
A heartbeat and seeming unimportant acts
 converge, steering fate—shaping lives,
 living rooms, and nations.

How much time do we have to discover
    who we are, where we are,
    and where we should be?
For time is too priceless to spill and squander,
    too fleeting, too precious,
    too pregnant to leave childless!

Dear God, may I make all seasons springtime.
May I birth its pains and passions slowly,
    squeezing out its childhood, taking time to dance and sing,
    to give and take, to share one's love, one's life.
Time to heal and harvest, time to remember and rejoice.
Time to forgive, to forget, to move on,
    to promise once again
    —to dream and live the dream.

May I fill each year, each day,
    each minute with abundant living.
May I walk in the present—not in the past.
May I plan for tomorrow and live for today!
May I stretch each waking moment
    —wring each sweeping second dry
    drop by precious drop and drink deeply
    while it is yet day.

Here and Now

Where have all the years gone?
Parenting a blur.
Fuzzy images of five in the car,
    sweltering summer sun,
    waves of heat rising off the highway,
    no air-conditioning and three little girls in seat belts.
"Are we there yet?"
    —fifteen minutes after leaving,
    a thousand miles to go.
What happened to the birthday cakes,
    the board games, kids sleeping over,
    fish 'n chips on Friday night, paycheck permitting;
    that first high-school dance, that first off-center kiss?
Seems like only yesterday?
No, seems like never
    —almost squeezed from memory.
Everything on fast forward
    like faded photographs
    scattered into the now!

Where have the years gone for you, Jesus?
Kicking stones on dusty roads,
dried fish, hard bread, curious crowds
    listening to the latest, folding back into what was.
Friends who aren't friends.
Stretched on a tree between strangers.
"Are we there yet?"
    —fifteen minutes on a cross
    a thousand miles to go.
Seems like only yesterday.
Seems like eternity.
Well, whatever happened left an empty tomb,
    a neatly folded cloth,
    and breakfast in Galilee.
Resurrection not *there* and *then*
    but *here* and *now.*
"Are we there yet?"
Sometimes.

Good Enough to Be True*

Is life *good enough to be true,*
too good to be true, or *not good enough to be true*?
It depends upon one's attitude, God.
When life is *good enough to be true*
    we accept things as they are without undue
    complaints, but also without great expectations.
How sad to live without great expectations.
Life that is *good enough to be true*
    holds little hope, no beckoning finger,
    no unexplored horizons.
Its contentment breeds apathy.

When life is *too good to be true*
    we view life with suspicion and cynicism . . .
Enjoy it while you can! You're in for a fall!
Things are going too well, this will never last!
Don't risk, don't trust, be on your guard!
Life that is *too good to be true*
    sows seeds of despair and pessimism.

When life *isn't good enough to be true*
    we see life with double vision.
We see things and people not only as they are
    but as they could be.
When life *isn't good enough to be true*
    we want to make life as true as it can be,
    as true as it should be.

Help me, God, to see things clearly as they are
    but not as final verdict.
Help me, God, to view life with healthy
    suspicion that resists cynicism and apathy.
Help me, God, to have double vision;
    to see life as it appears to be
    and as you would have it be.
Grant me courage to escape complacency,
    to make my life—
Good enough to be true!

*Written in response to a sermon by Rev. Dr. Maurice Boyd

Life Is Always Lived at the Edges . . .

We are but a heartbeat away from life or death, yet despite this reality we trundle through time unwittingly spending its gift like foolish billionaires. Youth persuades us that mortality belongs to *someone else.* No invoice outstanding. No end in sight. But as the clock ticks away the years, mortality knocks more feverishly on our door and takes up residence where down deep inside we knew it would. Neither friend nor foe, mortality moves in as welcome as a junkyard dog nipping at our heels near life's finish line. Like an unwanted roommate, this interloper points to the calendar, reminding us the rent is soon due.

Is life then merely a beginning, middle, and an end? No. The infant dies to the schoolchild, the schoolchild to puberty, the teen to adulthood. The problem is we think we live and *then* we die—when in fact—living and dying go on simultaneously. Every day we are coming alive, and every day we are dying a death. We see it in the death of winter, the birth of spring. Death and resurrection happen seasonally, daily, hourly, minute by minute, second by second—and life at *every age* can be filled with wonder.

As a youth I recall well-intended adults encouraging me to make the best of this period of my life. "Don't waste your youth—it's the best time of your life!" I didn't and it wasn't. If their admonishment was true, it held little promise for the future. It was like saying, "Sorry, everything is downhill from here." That's not true, of course. As I approach my senior years, life continues to get better! It's not what life makes of you; it's what you make of life. It has a lot to do with seeing God's loving touch in shadow as well as sunshine. The point is—*all life's seasons are graced by God's hand.*

All Seasons of Life Are Graced by God's Hand

(*Suggested tunes:* I Love Thee or St. Denio 11.11.11.11.)

1. All seasons of living are graced by God's hand
    From springtime of childhood to winter's short span.
    In sacred community differences bless
    And blend young and old in the faith they confess.

2. Delight in the treasure of children and youth;
    Probe deeply their questions—hear wisdom and truth.
    Respond to their need to be loved and to grow
    And nurture their dreams on the path as they go.

3. Remember the aged whose faith has held fast—
    Through sunshine and shadow and doubts
        that have passed.
    Give heed to their counsel for they have come through
    And walked living scripture with all whom they knew.

4. Rejoice that each gift seeks to honor God's Son.
    Be tender, be caring, embrace all as one.
    From smallest to largest, the least plays a part
    In shaping life's purpose to mirror God's heart.

At the Edge of an "Everyday Word"

Sometimes life or death of a loving relationship dangles at the edge of an *everyday word.* Do we say "I love you" when it desperately needs hearing? Do we offer a word of encouragement, a word of praise, affirmation, a word of reconciliation, a word of acceptance to an ear hungry for its whisper? There are friends, loved ones, and strangers desperately clinging to the edges of life—teetering back and forth over the brink of despair for want of an *everyday word.* They sit across from us at the workbench. They sit at the boardroom table, the student desk, the serving counter. They're as close as the breakfast table. Their faces stoic. Their voices mute. Their hearts pounding. All the while, beneath a cloak of complacency they are leaning forward stretching and straining to hear that word. An *everyday word* just on the tip of the tongue. And sometimes *we need* to hear that word ourselves.

An Everyday Word

Like a word on the tip of your tongue.
An everyday word—a name?
    an adjective? an adverb?
Teetering just on the edge,
    but it *just* won't fall from your lips.
Oh, what is it? Come on now! Come on!
You know what it means! You use it all the time.
    —I hate when this happens.
It's right there! Right there on the tip of my tongue,
    but I can't scrape it off.
I can feel it but I can't find it.
A simple word, a small word with a life of its own,
    playing hide and seek in the cobwebs of my mind
    —teasingly close, unwilling to slip away
    from its comfortable cerebral cottage
    and saunter back where it belongs
    in my vocabulary.

Come out! Come out, wherever you are!
Please! Please, won't you hear me into speech?

Like a word on the tip of your tongue.
Not forgotten. Not hiding or unknown.
Not this time! It's the right word at the right time
    for the right person!
But you hold back—you bite down,
      you tighten your lips, lest it gets out there,
      and face it—you *really want it out there!*
There's heat in it! There's power and pleasure in it!
Set it free, fling it right out there
  furiously, feverishly, forcefully—gleefully!
No! Bite down! Bite down!
Like a word on the tip of your tongue
    that cuts and crushes, hurts, hits and runs.
Swallow it! Come on, get it down!
It will damage both of you. Leave it unsaid.
Listen now! Listen—to the unspoken word of your friend,
Please! Please, won't you hear me into speech?

Like a word on the tip of the tongue.
Never forgotten. Not hiding. Always known.
It's the right word at the right time for the right person,
Wanting to be said, desperate to be heard.
A simple word, a small word with a life of its own.
Listen to it. It has your name on it.
Please! Please, won't you hear me into speech?
There's heat in it. Hear it now . . .
"Forgiveness"
    —slipping so easily off the tip of God's tongue.

At the Edges of Terrorism

The events of September 11, 2001, are frozen in memory. A land and a people heretofore spared (for the most part) from the bloodbath of terrorism tragically experienced in lands afar were suddenly thrust over the edge of tranquility into a midnight of confusion and despair. *Where is God in all this? Where is faith? Where is prayer? Was God on duty? Why did one survive and another die? God taking sides? Some prayers heard—others not? What is my Christian response?* Such questions beg far more than the following provides. Whirling from the shock of this monstrous act, I shared the following thoughts with fellow ministers.

Reflections on Dark Tuesday

Within minutes of the events of dark Tuesday, millions of words had been spoken, written, translated, and transmitted electronically and in print. They flooded a nation and a world unable yet to grieve as it teetered on the frozen edge of shock. The unspeakable was spoken. The unbearable was borne. Now, in the natal hours of an aftermath yet to be determined, grayness of thought gives way to the cold reality that life shall never be the same again. How does one express the inexpressible—the unthinkable? But more important, how do we, as those called to be ministers of blessing—bless wounded souls and anxious hearts in moments of uncertainty? Perhaps at no greater time than this are we commissioned as apostolic witnesses, teacher-learners, spiritual companions, and pastoral presence. In the midst of uncertainty, we must stand as ministers of sanctuary for those seeking sanctuary of heart, mind, and soul, "to appoint unto them that mourn in Zion, to give unto them beauty for ashes, the oil of joy for mourning, the garment of praise for the spirit of heaviness" [Isaiah 61:3 KJV]. To do so, we must first sort through our own ashes, confront our own mourning, and come to terms with our own heaviness.

Like many of you, I have wrestled with raw and suppressed emotions during this time. I have retreated frequently to the computer keyboard, pounding out feelings *for my eyes only.* I have found myself suddenly in tears triggered by seemingly unrelated happenings—a phrase in a book, a child's face, a pause in the day's routine when uninvited video images flooded my consciousness. Pictures of human ammunition exploding into twin towers, penetrating a *thought-to-be* impregnable fortress of defense, and plowing a charred furrow into the fertile fields of Pennsylvania. Repeated images of crumbling walls and cascading souls swallowing those who came to save and succor in the wake of a billowing gray cloud of death. Played back over and over again! A disaster film somehow escaping celluloid; its repetition ironically desensitizing us to its reality. "At first I couldn't watch them," said one elementary school child, "but now I can. It doesn't bother me as much . . . and *that's* what scares me!"

Despite such horror, I know beyond a scintilla of doubt what my convictions are, what my faith dictates, what my mind says. *You are a member of a peace church! You preach and sing it! You are dedicated to the pursuit of peace, reconciliation, and healing of the spirit.* I can shout from street corner and pulpit admonitions against violence and retribution. I can express logically and clearly the hope of Christian peace—the call for compassion and understanding—the folly of victims becoming victimizers—the need for forgiveness. All of these tenets, indelibly me! Not a whisper of compromise or hesitation. Not a question of what I know to be right, what I believe as a Christian—as a minister of blessing! And yet . . . and yet, there's that still small voice. Not the still small voice of the Spirit. Not the soft whisper of the sacred but the still small voice of my frail humanity. A faint, hidden voice deep within my shadow side, the dark recesses of my soul, silently screaming for recompense, for retribution. And when the hammer falls—"*the rockets red glare, the bombs bursting in air,*"—will my protests be pure? Will I drop prayerfully and dutifully to my knees while something buried inside sounds a note of secret satisfaction? I hope not. I pray not. Accountability, *yes!* Justice, *yes!* But not on *my* terms. Not to satiate any desire for retaliation no matter how faint, how shadowy. But the thoughts *are* there, aren't they? They have been for me. Tucked safely away at the core of emotions, raw and ripped by cowardly acts. Birthed by the tragic loss of blameless lives, devastated families, and a nation on its knees. Birthed by the loss of innocence. And birthed by the confession that compassion is fired by proximity. Each day thousands of innocents die from hunger and disease in countries afar and fail to get my attention, let alone stir my passions.

But I have shared and shown too much. A letter that began as a word of encouragement for ministers has wandered instead down a path of personal processing and venting. As one given somewhat to "poetic" expression I fear the foregoing may have overstated my emotional journey—the self-talk one has (or should have) with his or her shadow side. Notwithstanding, coming to terms with one's disparate voices is its own blessing. For as implied at the beginning of this letter, before we can hear the pain of others, we must hear first our own pain, our own doubts, and our own uncertainties. Thank you for hearing mine.

Let me then address briefly the question I originally intended to explore. In the light of these tragic times, how do "ministers of blessing" bless in times of uncertainty? The answer of course is one you already know and one you are already exercising. When specific answers fail to emerge, we move out in faith with what is known and abide in faith's calendar, patiently awaiting the Spirit's guidance. In other words, we bless others by the certainties that claim us. By the certainties that sustain us. By the unshakeable certainty of One who stands with us in the dark night of the soul, who never flees, never abandons—who wraps us in the embrace of abiding grace in sunshine and shadow.

We bless through prayer—personal, private, one-to-one, and corporate. We bless through personal witness of God's message of hope and healing. We bless through the *ministry of presence* by visiting and by truly *being with* old and young. We bless by sharing candidly and honestly our own half-doubts and the clear and compelling witness that these are eclipsed by God's promises. We bless by helping others to "live in the light of their hopes and not the shadow of their fears." We bless by sustaining and supporting pastors and leaders. We bless by smiling and laughing again—for laughter opens the windows of the soul and allows the fresh air of freedom to fill our lungs and our lives. We bless by being there when others are not. We dispel fear with love and uncertainty with certainty. We bless by sharing who we are and what we have.

Near Yet Far

Engaged yet disengaged. Near yet far, real yet unreal.
Eyes and ears, millions—hearing yet not hearing, seeing yet not seeing.
Surreal images, unreal images.
Human missiles exploding into twin towers
     dispatching death across breakfast tables, office desks,
     barber chairs, and laundromats.
A nation crowded into one space, one place, one time,
     one fiery flaming hell frozen in the mind.
The living landscape of America squeezed into a video tube,
     catching its breath watching, waiting, wondering, wailing,
     "My God! My God!"
Silent screams near yet far, real yet unreal, engaged yet disengaged.

Hollow thoughts, dry tears. Blind eyes, deaf ears,
     minds that can't compute, words that can't be formed—
     sealed by shocked lips.
Faceless neighbors—sisters, brothers *"looking into the mirror for the last time,*
     dressing to die," waving good-bye or not good-bye
     to wives and husbands, friends and family,
     to laughing children forever young in their eyes.

I am a foreign national. A resident-alien. A visitor. No party allegiance. No voting rights. A Canadian, through and through. Deeply proud of my heritage, my culture, my country. But on Tuesday morning, I became an American. Not wrapped in the Stars and Stripes. Not right hand over the breast singing "God Bless America." Not red, white, and blue. Yet I became an American. On Tuesday morning the British became Americans. On Tuesday morning Australians became Americans. On Tuesday morning Mexicans, Germans, Russians, Italians, Africans—the peoples of France, Germany, Russia, India, Canada . . . became Americans. On Tuesday morning, lines of citizenship were erased. People with their own brand of "life, liberty, and the pursuit of happiness" folded flags, put away national anthems. On Tuesday morning—Americans wept and the human family tasted salt.

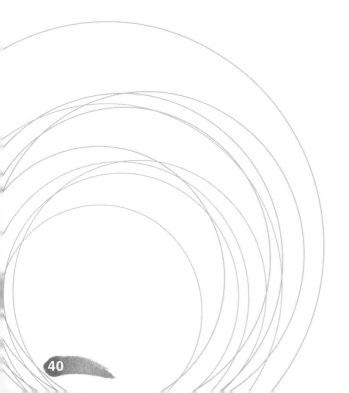

Gracious God, "Lift us up on eagles' wings"

    so you need not bend so low—to pour the balm of healing hope upon us.

"Lift us up on eagles' wings"

    that our catharsis may not flow in acts of hatred and revenge but spill out
    into rivers of love and compassion.

"Lift us up on eagles' wings"

    that we might follow he who was born in darkness and cradled
    in a feeding trough;
    he who brought life to death, stretched love upon a tree,
    and emptied cold tombs.

"Lift us up on eagles' wings"

    that we might rise again—restored, refreshed, renewed,
    filled with new hopes, new dreams, new visions of what it is
    to be your people.

"Lift us up on eagles' wings"

    that we might smile and laugh again, living your joy, living your peace,
    living your love.

Send us forth on wings of hope, dear God, our prayers lifting the lost and the
    losing, our feet marching on your path, our hands serving your will.

Lift us up, we humbly pray, in Jesus' name. Amen.

Part 3

Letting the Spirit Breathe Freely:
Prayer as Positive Disillusionment

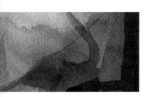

If prayer as death and resurrection is death of the old self and resurrection of a new self—it is *also* death of unhealthy intellectual perceptions *about* God and the birthing of a new relationship with God. It puts to death our illusions and resurrects us to reality. In other words, prayer can serve as a means for "positive disillusionment"—a release from the *immaculate perceptions* we hold near and dear. Our *ideas* of God are *not* God. God is bigger and better than our best expectations. When we let the Spirit breathe freely, we place no personal limits or restrictions on its power to bring new life to body, mind, and spirit. We breathe in. We breathe out. We take in the new and exhale the old.

Parker Palmer, in an article titled "The Monastic Way to Church Renewal," writes: "Remember that 'disillusionment' is a positive process in the spiritual life; it means losing our illusions so that we may come closer to reality." [7]

Prayer as cross is crucifixion of the intellect. It is putting to death the idolatry of knowledge. Our pursuit for understanding, our hunger for information, our straining at exegesis can be substitutes for God. Henri Nouwen in *The Way of the Heart* says that a viewpoint that restricts the meaning of prayer to thinking about God leads to frustration. God becomes a subject that needs to be scrutinized or analyzed. Nouwen says monologue prayers are "products of a culture in which high value is placed on mastering the world through the intellect."[8]

Ironically, theologians cannot pray and be theologians. Frequently theologians talk about God as though God were not present. Deity becomes "third person." It is easier to read, study, think, and talk about God than to commune with and experience God. Nouwen cautions that doing theology can make prayer impossible:

> Often it seems that we who study or teach theology find ourselves entangled in such a complex network of discussions, debates, and arguments about God and "God-issues" that a simple conversation with God or a simple presence to God has become practically impossible.[9]

Nouwen characterizes crucifixion of the intellect in softer terms. In *Reaching Out* he refers to our need for a "Poverty of Mind." He states, "Someone who is filled with ideas, concepts, opinions, and convictions cannot be a good host." He points out that poverty of mind is a spiritual attitude, a willingness to recognize the incomprehensibility of the mystery of life. Nouwen counsels: "To prepare ourselves for service we have to prepare ourselves for an articulate not knowing, a *docta ignorantia,* a learned ignorance."[10] For communion with God we must then be willing to crucify intellect, to empty ourselves so that we might receive.

Prayer as positive disillusionment offers a final resting place for those negative characteristics and traits that prevent us from being truly alive. Exposed to new understandings of self, we can bury old hurts, poor attitudes, destructive habits, and inflated self-conceptions. We move from the unreal to the real.

Determining the real from the unreal was no less easy for those who walked and talked with Jesus. The disciples were perplexed with life's uncertainties and asked, "Lord, teach us to pray." Can we reach God? Can we understand what it means to be God's person? Is religious faith an illusion? What is real and what is unreal? So many questions; so few solid answers.

Nouwen suggests we should not live in the answers of life but in the questions of life. He quotes the poet Rainer Maria Rilke:

Be patient toward all that is unsolved in your heart and . . .
try to love the questions themselves. . . . Do not seek answers
which cannot be given you because you would not be able to
live them. And the point is to live everything. Live the questions
now. Perhaps you will then gradually, without noticing it, live
along some distant day into the answer . . .[11]

Life is not fair. As much as we would like life's tragedies and per-
plexities to be resolved by neat and tidy answers, the reality is they may
not be. Prayer is not living the answers but living the questions. *Living*
questions *is* reality.

Someone has said, "That which is thought to be real will be real in its
consequences." Certainly this statement is not applicable to every situ-
ation. Several have skated through thin ice that was thought to be thick.
However, perceptions do color behavior. If God is thought to be transcendent, omniscient, omnipotent, distant, and unapproachable—prayer will
be next to impossible. Who can comfortably commune with a being so
remote and removed from flat tires, potholes, toothaches, and tragedies?
Such a God is unreachable and "unreal."

For Jesus, God was reachable and real. Jesus related to God not
primarily as omnipotent creator and sustainer, but as a loving intimate
parent. Not simply father but "Abba" meaning literally "Daddy." Jesus
said, "If you have seen me you have seen the Father." The mystery of the
Incarnation aside, Jesus demonstrated the reality of God's *personhood*.
He freed many from the disillusionment of a distant God exclusively
intimate with Abraham and the prophets—or a God who was on special
terms with the learned and wise Pharisees.

Jesus illuminated God as beloved parent. God as *person* brings Deity
as close as mother, father, children, friend, and stranger. Jesus at times
withdrew in prayer to Abba privately but lived a life of constant prayer.
He was continually aware of the faces of God in all those he saw. As
Mother Teresa has said, Jesus saw God in "all his distressing disguises."
God's *personhood* dispels illusions that God is far removed from this
life. Prayer as positive disillusionment gives us time to withdraw privately and confront our own personhood: "What are my disguises? Who *am* I
really? Who *are you*, God, and *where* do I see your face?"

Who Are You, God?

Who are you, God?
    and where are you when it's raining?
There is thunder in my life.
Engulfed by swirling, brooding clouds of doubt I scream your name.
But you are silent.
No answer comes from you amid the storm.
Where are you when it's raining?

Who are you, God?
    and where are you when emptiness invades?
There are tears that flow unseen
And deafening cries of anguish never heard.
Why are you silent?
No answer comes from you amid the void.
Where are you when emptiness invades?

Who are you, God?
    and where are you when death wins out?
Earthquake, wind, and fire claim young and old,
Bullets whine and cancer cheats us all.
Who's in charge and who's to blame?
You are silent.
No answer comes from you
    when death wins out.

Who are you, God?
Omniscient, omnipotent, eternal, and supreme?
We make you in our own image
    and are dismayed when you break the mold.
Trapped within the confines of our theology,
    you cry out!
But we are silent; no answer comes from us.
We cannot change a "changeless one"
    and remain unchanged ourselves.

Who are you, God?
You are the God beyond our God.
You are the God of surprises.
You are "New Being."

You are always more than we expect
　　　—more than our highest hope!
Your love is present in the silence;
　　　present in the laughter and the tears.
You weave your tapestry of life
　　　free of fairness or unfairness.
For your justice is beyond our justice,
　　　your understanding beyond our understanding.
You are mystery disclosed in humanity,
　　　subject to limits self-imposed.
You are Father, Mother, Child, Sustainer.
You are light and darkness,
　　　—the silence and the storm,
　　　—the healing and the hurt.
You dare to come unwelcomed.
You give and never take.
You risk and never sleep.

Who are you, God?
You are the old man on the park bench feeding pigeons,
　　　—the artist pouring himself onto canvas
　　　—the author spilling herself onto pages
　　　—the frightened teen doing drugs
　　　—the homosexual searching for self
　　　—the cat caught in a tree.
You are the crimson glow of sunset,
　　　the icy sting of winter wind.

Where are you when emptiness invades?
　　　—when death wins out?
Where are you when it's raining?
You are the rain!
You are the answer to our finitude.
You are life—you ARE!
　　　. . . It is enough.

Who am I, God,
　　　and where am I when it's raining?
Your still small voice replies:
"You are mine—You are with me;
　　　It is enough!"

Jesus—the Question

Bumper-sticker Christians say,
"JESUS IS THE ANSWER!"
Is he? I wonder. Is Jesus the answer
     or is Jesus the Question?
God, we want answers!
We want them tied up neatly and completely
     so that the questions go away.
Questions are disturbing!
They're so open-ended—*so unfinished*!
And yet . . . and yet questions can be so
     wonderful, so life giving, so enticing,
     so sweetly mysterious, *so necessary*.
They fly in the face of omniscience.

Omniscience is a god with no hills to climb.
Omniscience is Jesus pulled by strings,
     dancing toward Golgotha,
     every line rehearsed, every note on key,
     meeting no one for the *first* time.
Omniscience is a tragic Jesus.
 A Jesus who never doubts.
 An "All-Knowing-Jesus"
     —safe, secure—wrapped so tightly
      in divinity he's void of humanity.
     —a "Jesus Is the Answer" Jesus
      stripped of the sheer joy of wonder.
A life unexamined—a life not lived.

Thank you, God, for unfinished questions—
     for answers that satisfy *only* for the moment.
Thank you for wonder and wilderness,
     for marvel and mystery, for horizons that call.

Thank you for the riddle of grace,
  the vastness of space, the puzzle of being.
Thank you for your strange love wrapped up
  in a manager—a babe—a boy—a man
  bigger than slogans.
A Jesus making waves
  as well as calming seas.
A Jesus climbing hills, probing the darkness,
  searching his way!
Thank you for this *incomplete* Jesus,
  this *Jesus of Questions*
  —playfully sprinkling the salt of discovery
  on every bland soul including his own.
Thank God for Jesus
  —*both Answer and Question.*

Behind Fences

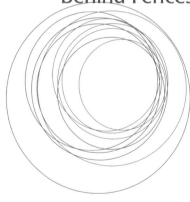

May I always question, ponder, and doubt.
May I look beyond the ranges,
  behind fences where trembling queries
  prick the heart and stir the soul.
May questions peal and purge,
  puzzle and probe.
May they pull with promise
  —stripped of fear and stuffed with wonder.
Stretch and disturb me, God.
Help me listen, wait, and wonder.
Call me far beyond the ranges.
Let me tear down all my fences.
Help me hold to who you are
  —and release who I'd have you be.
Perhaps then I shall know who I am
  and whose I am. Will I? I wonder.

Puzzles and Pieces

I remember when life was simple.
When everything had a place
    and it fit secure and contented.
It was a time when faith was "knowing,"
    and "knowing" demanded no risk.
God was in heaven
    and all was right with the world—
        and with me, because I *was* the world.
There was an answer for every question.
Even painful questions had simple answers
    "It's God's will!" "It's meant to be," or
    "There's a purpose to it."
Faith was secure, church was secure,
I was secure. It was a good time,
    a comfortable time, a time without risks, a simple time.

But it's different now.
The puzzle is broken—the pieces don't fit.
Assurance and security have naively knocked
    on doors and boldly entered rooms of new
    ideas and unasked questions.
And simplicity died.
What ever happened to the good old days?
To that old-time religion?
Was it good enough? Old enough? Gospel enough?
God, can I be comfortable in the "new"?
Secure in my insecurity? Assured in persistent doubt?
Can I learn to "live in the questions"
    as I once lived in the answers?

There's no turning back, God.
The old puzzle that *wasn't*—is gone.
I must find a new simplicity.
A simplicity of trust.
A willingness to knock on doors
    and enter rooms simply trusting you'll be there
    with some new piece of the puzzle,
    some new surprise that defies the definitions I've created.

The old simplicity stood firmly on solid
      answers, but the answers stood on trust.
The new simplicity stands on questions.
Ironically, the questions stand also on trust.

Help me, God, to be trusting.
Help me find a new simplicity.
To be as comfortable in "not knowing" as "knowing."
To permit the questions to find
      their own security, their own place.
To know, despite contradictions and
          complexities, that you are in your heaven
          and all is right with the world and with me,
          because I am a *part* of it.

Questions and Quarrels . . .

   Faith's journey is exciting and perplexing. It's a roller-coaster ride of ups and downs and twists and turns—a never-ending ride where questions dangle more often unresolved than resolved. I confess there have been times when I did not know what I believed—yet, there has never been a time in which I did not know in *Whom* I believed.

   If your God cannot surprise you, then your God is too small. As one writer expressed it, "Have a lover's quarrel with your faith." A lover's quarrel is like a storm at sea. At the surface the sky is inky black—lightning flashes, thunder rolls, winds howl, and waves explode. But beneath wind and wave, not far below foam and fury, the sea is calm and tranquil. There flows a deep, steady current of trust and love.

   I know there will be storms ahead—times when God will seem absent, dark nights of the soul, more twists and turns, and questions that beg solving. There will be quarrels with God and quarrels with self. And God will have quarrels with me. How will I respond to the deep queries that strain the soul—questions that have been placed in my keeping—*our keeping. Will people be valued above issues? Will peace replace war? Will freedom ring and food be shared? Will lines be erased and walls tumble down? Will theology become biography? Will love be lived?* These questions God cannot answer!

Can You Answer All Our Questions?
(*Tune:* Vesper Hymn 8.7 8.7 8.6.)

1. Can You answer all our questions?
   Can You see into the night?
   Do the maps of our conventions
   Circumvent Your probing sight?
   God of vision, boldly venture!
   Be set free from our confines!

2. Do our wants and whims besiege You?
   Can we hear Your plaintive cry?
   Can Your prayers find any venue
   That our actions soon deny?
   God who calls us, God who's waiting,
   Be set free from empty praise!

3. Are there limits to Your actions?
   Is there nothing You can't do?
   Do our prayers and incantations
   Find You lost for what to do?
   God who searches, God who questions,
   Be set free from polished lamps!

4. Please release us from the pleasure
   That a god of magic gives.
   Make us partners with full measure
   Blessing lives to fully live.
   God of vision, boldly venture,
   Set us free from our confines!

Part 4

Letting the Spirit Breathe Naturally:
Prayer as Unemployed Worker

Prayer can be hard work! It can be a struggle to find time to let the Spirit breathe naturally in our daily life. We've got places to go, people to meet, and things to do. When do you squeeze God in? There's not much provocation to put God on your Palm Pilot during fat times when all is well with the world—when the boss is happy, report cards are all "A's," the stock market is soaring, and life is a sunny 75 degrees. Prayer is hard work—no, more often it is no work at all when we have things well in control. Ironically, when life's bubble bursts, when times are thin not fat, even "parachute prayers" ("Bail-me-out, Jesus" prayers) can be hard work if we think we have to work at prayer.

Positive disillusionment releases us from the illusion of inflated self-reliance. In Isaiah's words we realize that "our righteous deeds are like a filthy cloth" (Isaiah 64:6 NRSV). We affirm the reality of our total dependence on the grace of God and the futility of "good works" as meritorious acts. All of life is gift. Regardless of how employed we may be in Christian service, work for God is God's work not our work. When we let the Spirit breathe naturally, that is, not forced and formulated, we become less employed with activities that actually crowd God out of our lives. Prayer invites us to become unemployed workers—to be less *self-employed* and more *God-employed*. Ironically, wasting time with God can be a struggle—plain hard work!

A young college student, deeply committed to her church and God, found herself confused and conflicted by what she feared was her eroding spiritual life. "I know what I must do," she said. "I know that I must discipline myself to read more scripture and to pray more but the more

I try the harder it gets. I can't seem to make it work anymore." The best advice I could give her was to stop trying. "Stop working at it, and stop beating yourself up because nothing seems to be happening." She needed (as do we all) to let the Spirit breathe—to relax, to give room for herself, and room for the Spirit to breathe naturally. She needed to become an unemployed worker.

Prayer as unemployed worker confronts us with a contradiction; we must work at not working at prayer. Henri Nouwen says, "The paradox of prayer is that we have to learn how to pray while we can only receive it as a gift." [12] He tells us that many have devoted years to faithful and strenuous "prayer work" only to declare they were as far from God as when they started. This does not suggest prayer is effortless. It means that fevered efforts to *discover* God can become ends in themselves; they can get in the way of God discovering us. "All mystics stress with an impressive unanimity that prayer is 'grace,' that is, a free gift from God, to which we can only respond with gratitude. But they hasten to add that this precious gift is within our reach." [13] It becomes reachable with the awareness that wasting time with God "just sitting there doing nothing" is time well spent.

Wasting time with God provides an open space—a freeing of the Spirit—that allows the fresh breath of heightened awareness to realign our priorities. Activities we think are real and very important become less real and less important. Prayer helps us to understand that activities performed in the name of God may replace association with God. We can be over-employed.

Caught up in good works to perform, appointments to be filled, meetings to attend, sermons to prepare, hospital visits to be made—we scarcely have time for ourselves let alone Jesus. Unconsciously we live out an unreal Christianity, which is nothing more than a theology of motion. It is cosmetic Christianity, which looks and feels good on the surface. Busyness can bankrupt us of Jesus' presence. Palmer describes this as "functional atheism":

> Many of us are guilty of "functional atheism." Though our language pays lip service to God, our actions assume that God does not exist or is in a coma. Functional atheism is the belief that nothing is happening unless we are making it happen. [14]

Whereas prayer ties us back to God, functional atheism pulls us away from God. Functional atheists become "persons *from* God." So distracted by peripheral pursuits, they drift far from true center. So busy sharing Jesus with others, they take little time with Jesus themselves. "Persons *from* God" try to outrun Jesus. Unfortunately, it is all too easy to become persons from God and persons of the god called "activity." Prayer as unemployed worker is an invitation to stop moving, to be less employed, and to be still and know that God is God. Nouwen says:

> The literal translation of the words "pray always" is "come to rest." The Greek word for rest is *hesychia*. . . . A hesychast is a man or a woman who seeks solitude and silence as the ways to unceasing prayer. The prayer of the hesychasts is a prayer of rest.[15]

Time is valuable yet we fail to take time to experience time. Every moment is so filled with doing and thinking that we never experience "being." How can God squeeze in between the competition? If time is a premium, why do we seldom schedule time with God? Is wasting time (even with God) unproductive? Apparently, we are convinced productivity is anathema to silence, contemplation, and being at rest. The Spirit cannot breathe naturally when we are forever on the run.

Outrunning Jesus

We are running, God. Running, running.
Outrunning Jesus! So little time, so much to do,
    so many good intentions never realized.
Grace us with emptiness, God.
Restore us with silence.
Help us waste time with you.
Free us from harried pursuits of permission.
Strip away our calendars, day planners,
    all-timers, *no-timers*—our plotting and planning
    in lieu of playing.
Grant us pause, dear God, so we may simply "be"
    and in "being" discover who we are
    and who we should be.
Bless us with a healthy ministry of absence
made possible by your ever-abiding presence.

Running on Empty

My mind is empty this morning
    as I contemplate this psalm.
How odd to be concerned
    about an empty mind.
Emptiness is a major achievement
    in this day and age when a mind must be
    full to the brim, crowded with yesterdays,
    todays, and tomorrows.

Always on the run, Lord.
Running desperately to catch up or keep up,
Scrambling a step ahead of the competition.
Running through moments of leisure,
    propped up in front of the TV,
    peering at the Internet, pouring through a
    novel, thumbing magazines.

Always on the run—running on empty.
Desperately filling space.
Anything to occupy a mind.
One must not sit idle.
Perish the thought a mind should be empty.
Perish the thought?
Good God, it's only when we do perish our thoughts
    we find a moment's peace;
    a quiet time, an empty time,
    a time to just "be."

Help me, God, to not fear emptiness.
Help me to stop running—
    to stop filling every moment and
    allow moments to fill me!
Help me find you in the quiet.
Help me celebrate the past, live the present,
    and anticipate the future as friend.
Mute the voices vying in my head.
Take me to a safer place
    where quiet can be fed.
Grant me pause.
Stop my feverish searching.
Allow me to be found by you.

Bliss

The poet-prophet said, *"Follow your bliss!"*
How sad, God, we try to create bliss rather than follow it.
We want to be happy.
We want life to be full, complete, satisfying.
We want security, success, status, and stability.
No surprises, please.
Unless, of course, they're on the plus side of the ledger
        —winning lottery tickets, unexpected promotions,
        pats of praise, kisses on the cheek, nods of approval.
Such blissful envoys.

But what *is* bliss?
Something that comes to us
        or something we come to?
An emotional rush,
        a "high" that teases, then flees?

You've said, *"We are that we might have joy!"*
You've said your joy could remain in us, our joy could be full.
Surely such joy, such bliss, is not
        something that happens, but something we become
        —something within us, something we are—*authentically*.

Strip away our veneer, God,
        our innate propensity to define bliss on our terms,
        our tendency to wait for wonders where wonders abound,
        unnoticed, unheard, unseen, unrealized.
Help us to stop shooting for the stars.
Help us see them.

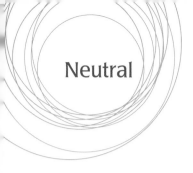

Neutral

I'm feeling neither happy nor sad today.
But as I think of life
     I can't help wonder if there isn't a place
     or a time to be *neutral*.
Sometimes we're so busy, God,
     we take no time to *take time*
     —time with self and time with you.

Silence the clock in my head.
Close my day planner.
Put deadlines to death.
Help me, God, to take time.
Time for nature. Time for leisure.
Time for emptiness. Time for you.
May being replace doing!
May silence fill sound!
May I celebrate the luxury and blessing of a
     sweet breath of neutrality
     so that feeling neither happy nor sad
     has its own safe place.

The List

Just added to THE LIST and already in arrears!
Wasn't there yesterday!
Stares at me like a promise broken
     before formed or thought of.
Says, *"One for today and one for the day before."*
"Double up, you can do it—make the list happy!"
"Make it up! Catch it up! Get it done!"
This retroactive resolution scampering
     to fill the past with the present,
     now captive to the list!

Another greased-ball-bearing year
     careening down a spiral trough.
Didn't see it coming—didn't see it pass.
Was I on it or under it?

Christmas, New Year's come and gone
Glorious resolutions punched out on a keyboard.
THE LIST—lose weight; exercise; take time off;
  set goals and objectives; actually *read those*
  books I just "had" to add to my library.
Upright books—silent sentinels standing still
  uncracked, unconsummated,
  —inky words of wisdom, tight, together,
  unturned, unseen,
  —muted landscapes, life-changers,
  poetry and prose,
  trapped between pages
  gasping for air, light, and appropriation.
Yes, put them on THE LIST!
This list of great expectations couched in little victories
  —tiny anticipated achievements forging a new me.
Reasonable, manageable, *workable*
  (and *that's* the enemy).
Discipline, God, discipline. Isn't that what it's about
  —taking one's measure, stretching it,
  straining it, discovering *more* soul?
Yes! Put soul on the *the list—daily prayer;*
  daily music; daily meditation;
  daily silence (if I can find some); *daily study*
  —and oh yes— the "new one," a daily psalm.
Daily! That's the key! Check them off,
  each day, every day!
It's so good to check things off, God.
Ah! There's the rub, isn't it?
Because checked off prayers
  are prayers "checked off."
Passionless, programmed piety
  like a kiss over the telephone.
My "eight o'clock with Jesus."
My God-time "over and out"!
Cross it off—uncommitted, unconsumed,
  incomplete, ineffectual.
Dear God, save me from THE LIST!

Part 5

Breathing for One's Self:
Prayer as Positive "Selfness"

No one can do your breathing for you. It is an involuntary life-giving action that goes on second for second unnoticed and unacknowledged until the oxygen that feeds our blood cells is suddenly in short supply or not available at all. Others can aid your breathing. The miracles of modern medicine can mechanically provide air to your lungs, but the rest is up to you. It's a self-centered, life-sustaining activity. Certainly not one that we deem "selfish" with all the negative baggage this term conveys. Similarly, only you can allow the Spirit to breathe new life in you, for this, too, is a self-centered decision. Stripped of the guilt so often associated with centering on "self," we can discover through prayer the positive side of selfishness. (The word "selfishness" reaps such offensive connotations I am tempted to substitute a non-word, "selfness," in its place).

We need a healthy self-centeredness—a holistic "selfness." We've been conditioned to view self-centeredness and selfishness in negative terms. Jesus said to love your neighbor *as* yourself, not *more than* yourself. We need to care for ourselves. The same velocity of activities that preempts time spent with God, preempts time for needed self-care. There is a positive, healthy side to selfishness. It is stewardship over the gift of one's own life. Anthony Bloom in his classic *Beginning to Pray* states we begin by addressing prayer inward:

> Where should I direct my prayer? The answer I have suggested
> is that we should direct it at ourselves. Unless the prayer which
> you intend to offer to God is important and meaningful to you
> first, you will not be able to present it to the Lord.[16]

We not only need time for ourselves; we desperately need to discover who we are and whose we are. Many people are not on good terms with themselves because they don't know who they are. This is not a form of schizophrenia; rather, it is failure to come to terms with our humanity and our divinity. Bloom admonishes, "If we cannot find the kingdom of God within us, if we cannot meet God within, in the very depth of ourselves, our chances of meeting Him outside ourselves are very remote." [17]

The gospel is the right arrangement of relationships. The good news brings rebirth to fractured or strained relationships with the past, present, and future. Marginalized relationships with family, friends, others, and God can be restored in response to the gift of grace. This response begins with self-discovery, self-care, and self-acceptance.

Acceptance

How does one truly accept oneself?
God, you've made it clear that you accept us!
Even as the hymn says, *"just as we are."*
You know us better than we know ourselves.
You see the good, the bad, the ugly,
     our plastic virtues—strings attached.
How do *you* accept the unacceptable?

Help me, God, to accept me as I am.
Not an acceptance that defeats desire nor
     strangles hope to be *more* than I am
     —but acceptance that fills weakness with
     strength and scales the heights of promise!

Help me build on what you've given me,
     free of sluggish and blinding remorse.
Help me put yesterday with yesterday,
     today with today, and see each morning as promise.
May I receive each new day as gift,
     pregnant with possibilities, brimming with freshness,
     crowded with acceptance of others and *self.*

Nobody Loves You Like You Do

Nobody loves you like you do!
How do I love me? Let me count the ways—
"Brash," you say? *"Arrogant! The height of conceit!"* you say?
Not really. Just the plain unvarnished truth.
NOBODY loves you like *you* do!
Nobody *knows* you like *you* do.
Nobody lives with you 24/7—like *you* do!
Nobody hears the silent shouting
     —the beefs, the bouquets, the litanies of assessment,
     —that animated measuring rod distorting victories and failures
     —all that self-talk like whispers in the wind.
So hear this! It's something you already know:
     "Nobody, I mean *nobody,* loves you like *you* do!"

Sorry, God, step aside for a minute, this is personal, private stuff
     between me and . . . well, *me.*
Right! I know—You'll eavesdrop anyway.
You'll end-up telling me
     I am neither as bad nor as good as I think I am.
One dose of humility and divine acceptance coming up:
     Self-love—grace-filled—unmade-to-measure—any-size-will-do—
     you're-worth-everything-along-with-everyone-else agape love.

Look! I know You.
Before I abort these rambling thoughts,
You'll find some way to remind me that at the end of the day
     (*as well as the start of it*) nobody loves me like You do.
See! You've already done it!
You've ruined the whole game.
You've put my stream-of-consciousness writing on freeze frame.
Back off, God! Indulge me a little!
Let me continue to say the obvious unabated.

If I don't love me, can I really love another?
If I don't love me, can I really love life?
If I don't love me, can I really love at all?
If I don't love me, who will?
That's your cue, God . . . I'm waiting,
Go on, say it, I really need to hear it.
"Nobody loves you like I do!"

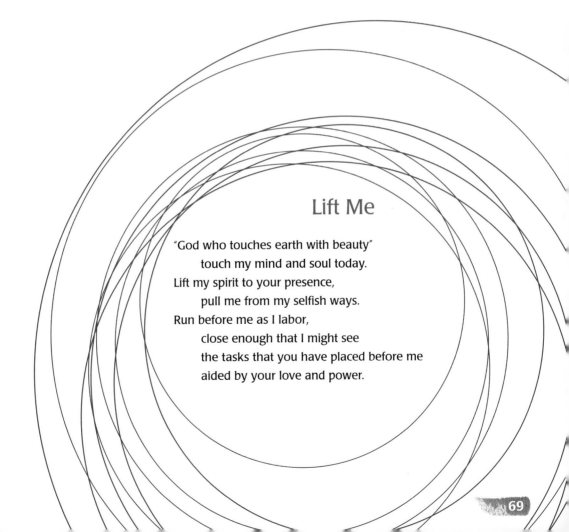

Lift Me

"God who touches earth with beauty"
    touch my mind and soul today.
Lift my spirit to your presence,
    pull me from my selfish ways.
Run before me as I labor,
    close enough that I might see
    the tasks that you have placed before me
    aided by your love and power.

I'm Here, I'm Real!

"Have a good day! Good to see you!
We must get together! Take care. God bless!"
Innocent phatic phrases cloaked in familiarity,
      saying nothing—saying *everything*
      —reaching out between the lines:
"Notice me, look at me, I'm here, I'm real!"

Have I got your ear, God? Do you have mine?
There you are leaning forward hoping for a word,
      straining for some notice—a wink, a wave,
      a nod of recognition, a quick, *"Have a good day!*
      Good to see you! We must get together! Take care, God."

"Listen, child! Can you hear ME?
Scrambling in the traffic, screaming in the crowd,
      weeping in the shadows, laughing in a child?
      We really must get together.
      —Notice me, look at me, I'm here, I'm real!"

Played-out and Prayed-out!

It's Sunday morning. I'm sitting in Carolyn's "lectio divina" class. She wants each of us to write a psalm and I don't want to play. I'm psalmed-out, prayed-out, journaled-out. Not wanting to be seen as not participating (image is everything), I'll play anyway—and nothing's happening.

The words won't come this morning, God.
It's like they left me—found another home.
It's been a heavy week.
People have died and I've cried.
Look, I've been writing and praying all week.
I'm tired of praying,
     tired of playing priest, tired of sifting
     hope through sands of despair.
So let me drink a little emptiness.
Not neutrality—*emptiness*—
  a space and time to lay it down, to "just be"!
Not struggling to express the inexpressible.
Not working to formulate thoughts and feelings.
Just time out. Let me be.
Sometimes enough is enough!
Sometimes a breath of inactivity
     can be its own sweet breeze of healing.
Sometimes being alone—devoid of doctrines,
     stripped of sayings, slogans, scripts, and scriptures
     —is all I want.
Right now, I just want to put it all on the shelf
     and *you along with it, God.*
Tell you what!
Just let me be and I'll let you be.
     —You won't, of course
     . . . but then, neither will I.

God's Investment

Do not demean the Master
    with your cries of inadequacy.
Do not belittle his sacrifice with your cries of unworthiness.
Have you not cast your eyes to the heavens,
    and beheld the outline of a star?
Have you not basked
    in the gold of a radiant sunset,
    held a blade of grass, touched a leaf,
    and seen the dew upon the roses?
Your ears have caught the songs of birds
    and shared the cords of symphonies.
And are you not more than all of these?
For you are called to serve him.
He knows your limitations, your fears, your tremblings.
He has called you in weakness
    that you might become strong in him.
You are called with his calling . . .
To bring light to those in darkness,
    deliverance to those in bondage,
    and hope to those who have no hope.
You are a sacred trust,
A recipient and translator of his love.
You are God's investment.

Part 6

The "Being" and "Doing" of Breathing:
Prayer as Passive Voice

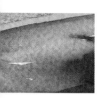

Some years ago I organized a staff meeting at a Benedictine monastery for a number of ministers for whom I had supervisory and leadership responsibility. We met to conduct necessary business, but our primary goal was spiritual refreshment—time to waste with God. Surprisingly, in some ways, it was not an easy transition. "Type A" personalities are by nature focused on "doing" (getting things done and done well) as opposed to "being" (emptying the self and being refreshed by God's Spirit without deadlines to meet and goals to achieve). It is a challenge for high-energy people to be less active and more passive—to receive instead of giving and gaining. Yet the gospel begins with receiving.

Christian ministry and service is too often thought of in the active voice. Prayer reminds us that the gospel begins in the passive voice. In other words, Christianity is not something we do, Christianity is something *initially bestowed.* The doing cannot precede the being. We rush into the mode of doing the gospel before receiving the gospel. It is not what we are doing for Jesus, but what Jesus has done and is doing for us. Trying to live out the gospel exclusively in the active voice is as futile as trying to eat tomorrow's leftovers today. Many "people of God" attempt to walk the second mile not having walked the first. Jesus often withdrew to gain strength and perspective in prayer. He could not always be "doing"; he needed time for simply "being."

Letting the Spirit breathe, then, is time for being. It is not an escape from life or a denial of work to be done. It is not a retreat from the world but a retreat for the world. Prayer reveals that all things are spiritual; it reveals that the universe is the arena of God's investment. Nothing is so secular that it cannot be made sacred.

What about the doing of the gospel? Should we not be about God's business? Prayer as "passive voice" empowers us to act. Some have seen contemplation and prayer as mystical diversions of piety. Prayer is not a means to deter doing or a replacement for social action. Prayer *is* action. The war between "pietist" and "activist" is a non-issue. Communion with a God whose love is unconditional, uncaused, uncalculated, and unrelenting can only be manifest in prayer that activates, not stagnates. Such prayer calls us to be and calls us to do. Being precedes doing; the doing of the gospel flows out of our intimate relationship with the One whose gospel it is.

Prayer is not a spiritual anesthetic or a denial of the unevenness of life. It does not keep pain away. Nouwen says prayer is far from sweet and easy. Often it will take us where we do not want to go. He refers to two contrasting incidents in the life of Jesus—the transfiguration on Mount Tabor and the agony in the Garden of Gethsemane. Nouwen writes, "When we have seen God in his glory we will also see him in his misery, and when we felt the ugliness of his humiliation we also will experience the beauty of his transfiguration."

Bloom counsels us that prayer empowers us to live the hurts and challenges of the Christian life:

> We must each take up our own cross, and when we ask something in our prayers, we undertake by implication to do it with all our strength, all our intelligence and all the enthusiasm we can put into our actions . . . we do it with all the power which God will give us.[18]

Prayer as "passive voice" realigns our priorities; it makes us keenly aware of God's love and action in our lives. Prayer's "passive voice" repeatedly tells us that we can only become doers of the gospel by becoming empowered receivers of the gospel. How easy it is to forget that God is giver and we are receivers.

How Easy It Is

How easy it is—to forget you, God,
    to live as though I were the center
    with you but a convenience in time of trouble.
How easy it is—to go through the motions:
mouth the right words, sing the right hymns,
pray the right prayers, visit families, pay tithes,
toss a buck to the homeless.

How easy is it for you, God?
To call with no response, to hold and not be held,
to pray and not be heard, to wait in the shadows,
    assigned to the background,
    giving all, receiving little?

Help me, God, to slip in behind you
    so I can mouth the right words,
    sing the right hymns, pray the right prayers,
    visit families, pay tithes—with *you* at the center,
    free of my shadow,
    released from the background.
Keep reminding me that life is gift
    and you are its giver.
Oh, to be a gracious receiver.
    —How easy it could be.

How Do You Bless God?

"Bless the Lord, O my soul, bless your holy name . . ."
How does one bless God?
Can I add to your greatness?
Can deeds or words of praise
  make you more than you are?
I give you only what is yours.

How does one bless God—giver of all that is given?
Perhaps I can bless your hidden presence,
        the "you" resident in each person
        —parent or child, prince or pauper,
        saint or sinner—these hidden faces of God.
But must I look for your presence
        in order to bless them?
Must I bless them because they are yours
        —because they *are* you?
Or can I learn to bless them for the sake of blessing?
Giving for the sake of giving.
Hoping for the sake of hope.
Loving for the sake of love.

Can I bless as you bless? Preveniently,
        conveniently, grace-fully?
Love without strings. Hope without handouts.
Can I bless as you bless?
Free of recompense, gift-given
        —agenda free, stripped of self,
        no thought of personal gain.
Is this not how you bless me, God?

How then does one bless God?
By fully receiving!
Invoice free, no points earned, no deeds done!
Graciously *received*, graciously *lived*!
Now, that is "Blessing the Lord, O my soul!"
                    Amen

For Gratitude, Not for Granted

Another day filled with possibilities, God,
     how wondrous to be alive!
I praise your name for all that is!
Yet even as I lift my heart in thanksgiving
     my tainted praise takes much for granted
     —sunsets unnoticed, colors unseen,
     landscapes unvisited.
Help me see beyond the obvious.
Help me hear the beauty of silence
     —the subtle, unlistened-to symphonies
     around and within.
Help me feel and sense the miracle of creation
     beyond the center of self.
Stir my soul! Awaken my joy!
Color my grayness of thought
     that I may take life for gratitude
     and not for granted.
Help me this day to not stray
     too far from *wonder.*

Part 7

Letting the Spirit Be at Home:
Prayer as Hospitable Host

We have already discussed the necessity of having a healthy self-centeredness—a willingness to accept that God has not only created us and continues to sustain us, but that God's Spirit dwells within us. A healthy sense of self allows us to unpack our bags. It is the doorway to our relationship with self and state before God. God patiently waits for us to acknowledge we are God's children and to accept ourselves regardless of warts and wrinkles, as "Abba" accepts us. Parker Palmer states, "Until we are at home with ourselves our relations with others will be distorted and distorting."[19] We feel at home when we are in an atmosphere of hospitality. Prayer, then, must be a "hospitable host."

Hospitality is defined as friendly and liberal reception of guests or strangers. It is the creation of free and friendly space. Hospitality provides an atmosphere of welcome and acceptance that invites naturalness. It is a warm openness—free of hidden agendas and protectiveness. It allows the Spirit to *be the Spirit*. Nouwen says that in the context of hospitality, guest and host can reveal their most precious gifts and bring new life to each other.

Prayer as "hospitable host" is coming to yourself and coming home. "Very often one says, 'O God bless me,' and having got the blessing we act like the prodigal son—we collect all our goods and go to a strange country to lead a riotous life." [20]

Scripture records that while feeding swine the prodigal son "came to himself." This event is not described as being an act of prayer, but certainly as he considered his plight and admitted his foolish behavior, he was in an attitude of deep contemplation. He had not been his "true" self but a false self, and he felt the urge to be at home. Prayer, then, is coming home. We, too, are often in a far country even in the guise of Christian service.

Prayer as hospitable host is not communing with the prime mover or the ground of all being. There is little hospitality in these impersonal labels. Prayer is an expression and experience of intimacy. Hospitality is not impersonal and functional; it is relational. Bloom says, "Prayer begins at the moment when, instead of thinking of a remote God, 'He,' 'The Almighty,' and so forth, one can think in terms of 'Thou.'"[21]

Bloom suggests we find a nickname for God—one that has personal meaning. We do not relate to close friends and loved ones by formal titles. We are often on "first name," even *special* name, basis. Bloom's idea of a nickname for God is not an attempt to be cute or demeaning but is a natural expression of hospitality, true devotion, and friendship. Bloom is saying we need to make friends with God and to share openly, trustfully, honestly, and candidly.

The challenge of this relational communion is not in exposing oneself to God; we are always exposed to God. The challenge is self-exposure while in the acknowledged presence of God. It is pulling back the curtains, opening the blinds, looking into rooms that have been tightly closed, and discovering the gift of God's grace.

Being at home means being present with God. Taking time for silence, listening to God's voice, however it may be expressed, is being present. We are sharing time with a friend. There is no need for artificial conversation at home. Relationships with loved ones always go beyond the surface. It is rooted in mutual hospitality and love, not exploitation. Similarly, prayer is free and friendly space, with no demands; it is not merely an opportunity to present a shopping list of petitions.

Prayer life focused exclusively on petition makes God a cosmic Santa Claus. Such a limited prayer perspective puts God at our disposal. If our relationship with God is centered primarily in God as provider, our prayers will increase or decrease in direct ratio to perceived needs or anxiety. We become very pious in times of crisis, and prayers become parachutes. How tragic it is when God doesn't bail us out or answer our petitions as we think best. Why, we wonder, is God never around when needed? What kind of a host is never at home? God has an absentee problem. We frequently pray that God will be present with us when it is *we* who are absent. Bloom graphically places this in perspective:

> But what about the twenty-three and a half hours during which God may be knocking at our door and we answer "I am busy, I am sorry" or when we do not answer at all because we do not even hear the knock at the door of our heart, of our minds, of our conscience, or our life. So there is a situation in which we have no right to complain of the absence of God, because we are a great deal more absent than He ever is.[22]

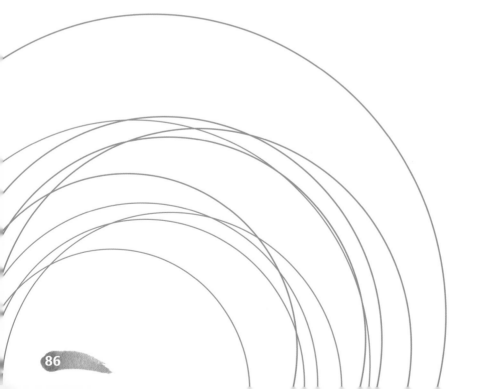

Homesick

Someone said, "The eyes are the windows of the soul."
What of those who have no eyes
    with which to see and be seen?
How is a soul discerned?
Is not its presence boldly seen and heard
    in actions done and words spoken?

Someone said, "There's no going home again."
What of those who have no home;
    no sweet memory, no warm retreat?
Is not home where one is?
Must we always search for sanctuary
    in hidden past or yearned-for future?
Can home for one, be home for all?

Someone said, "God is love."
But what of those who know no love,
    no gentle touch, no warm embrace?
What soul is resident behind their eyes?
What hope of home calls them?

Someone said, "Who is my mother, my brothers, my sisters?"
—and someone answered, *"Everyone!*
Everyone seeking hearth and home and heart.
Everyone homesick for your love!"
Was it *me*, Lord? Is this *my* answer?
Keep my shades open, God,
    so that through my eyes
    you can see and be seen.
Keep my ears alive to hear you
    where you dare not speak.
Help me touch and be touched.
Help me to be at home where I am,
    yet always homesick for the home
    you'd have me reach.

Homecoming:
Reflections on Rembrandt's
Return of the Prodigal Son

While attending a weekend retreat in Portland, Oregon, partici-
pants were assigned various scripture texts on which to medi-
tate and journal. My scripture was the story of the bent-over
woman, found in Luke 13. Our task was to pray the scriptures
(similar to lectio divina) that is, to read the text over several
times—not with an eye to interpret contextual meaning—but to
be grasped by any thought or message the text might have for
us as we meditated upon it. As I read and re-read the scripture
one phrase continually reverberated in my mind . . . "And a
woman was there." This made little sense to me; nevertheless
the words persisted. Having recently heard a testimony refer-
encing Rembrandt's Return of the Prodigal Son, *I remembered*
that the artist had painted the barely visible figure of a woman
standing in the upper left-hand corner. She is all but lost to the
background—a lonely solitary soul on the fringes of celebration
and homecoming. The following flowed out of my reverie.

And a woman is there—subtly, silently standing in the shadows.
A woman is there, undefined, shrouded in murky hues of muted light,
    stripped of self, her smudged soul bleeding with the background.
Search carefully—*a woman is there,*
    unacknowledged, undesired, disconnected, peripheral.
A woman is there—*just beyond the homecoming.*

A prodigal is there—recalcitrant, reclaimed, one shoe on, one shoe off,
    dust discarded, lost for gain of raced return.
Head bowed, kneeling, pregnant for welcome's healing word.
A prodigal is there—family, workers, friends, clustered so
    to celebrate the lost as found made sweet by father's long embrace.

But look once more—back behind the crowd
    a woman is there—somewhere in the silence,
    hungering for a word, a touch, a wisp of warmth.
    A woman is there—*just beyond the homecoming.*

A father's there—breathless down the path,
    pursuing fractured faith—a child returned on wings of hope.
A mother's there—unrelenting, unforgetting, unyielding to the breech,
    joy's blinding tears confirming heartache's plea.
A brother's there—his torn response entwined with love and hate.
A ring, a robe, a fatted calf, the picture seems complete.
Not quite—*There! There!* Almost out of sight
    a woman is there—nameless in the night,
    straining at the edges, fading from the scene.
    A woman is there—*just beyond the homecoming.*

A middle-aged man is there—unemployed, shattered home,
    tattered dreams.
A child is there—long hard nights, cold dark alleys,
    auctioned cheap to strange men in strange rooms.
An executive is there—Armani suits, sleek black cars,
    blue chip stocks and blue chip soul.
A lesbian is there—prisoner to self, screaming to get out,
    mute to family, friends, and faith.
A four-year-old battling leukemia, an elderly woman on Social Security,
    a teenage mother working two jobs . . .
Many faces, many races—
    not quite white enough, not quite tall enough, thin enough,
    smart enough.
Faceless faces translucent in the night, pushed to the edges—not quite
    in the picture.
Look again! *There! There!* Can you see them?
They're *all* there—WAITING—*just beyond the homecoming.*

Time Not Wasted . . .

The metaphorical images of prayer as death and resurrection, positive disillusionment, unemployed worker, positive selfishness, passive voice, and hospitable host are by no means exhaustive. Matthew Fox's definition of prayer as radical response to life hints at the breadth of possible illustrative images to which prayer and its benefits could be compared. They are as broad as life itself. But to what end? It is important to remember Nouwen's caution that arguments about God and "God-issues" can make a simple conversation with God or a simple presence to God practically impossible. In other words, there is ultimately greater value in being at prayer than in attempting to describe or define it. Said another way, wasting time with God is not time wasted.

Prayer, of course, is both private and corporate. One can "be at prayer" in sharing the hopes, dreams, aspirations, and prayerful expressions of others. I hope the personal psalms, prayers, and pieces in this work have not found you simply reading another's spiritual quest but deeply engaged in your own.

In many ways, prayer in its myriad forms and expressions is an exploration to find one's *true home*—a sense of *hospitality* and *unity* with the transcendent—a "lover's quarrel" with the struggles of immanence—and a place of peace amid life's ambiguity, pain, and startling joys. This is the heartbeat of prayer as "hospitable host." I chose this as my concluding metaphor because too often we are displaced persons, resident-aliens in search of sanctuary—that home where each soul is of inestimable worth and all share equally the role of host and guest. Hospitality is not exclusively focused on giving but also on receiving. True hosts must be willing to be guests—to share joyfully the gifts and graces of those they host. In prayer we need to feel at home, and God needs to feel at home. It must be a home where there is no shortness of breath for host or guest—a place, a condition, and a process that "lets the Spirit breathe!" Can we find this home?

Can We Find a Home?

Can we find a home of peace and grace
Where false veneers of place and race
Are stripped away from ev'ry face,
And old and young and weak and strong
Sing sacred songs of God's embrace?
Can we find this home?

Can we find a home where wars will end,
Where children play and wounds will mend,
Where laughter's balm pours hope on dreams,
Where weapons rust for want of schemes,
And violence dies and justice streams?
Can we find this home?

Can we find a home where faith's aflame
Where God is called by many names,
Where mosque and pew have equal claim,
And bread and wine and paschal lamb
Join incense burnt and whirling dance?
Can we find this home?

Can we find this home that's birthed within,
Where God resides, where love begins—
Where Spirit melts the frozen heart,
Where Love unites what's torn apart,
A home for all who seek God's heart?
We can be this home!

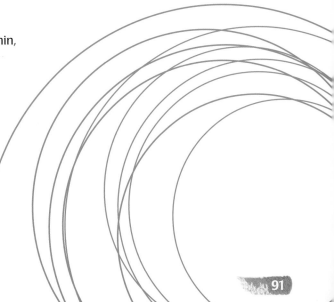

Afterword

At the outset of this collection I commented on how fitting it was that the ancients correlated the wind with the mystery of God. The wind is invisible. It comes from nowhere and goes where it wills, betraying the most sophisticated *Doppler radar*. Who has not been fooled by, blessed by, or for that matter, defeated by the wind? And who has not questioned the mystery of life—the coming and going of existence? We wrap this mystery around One whom we say is wholly other, transcendent, and immanent. The God who is here, yet *more than* here—the One who is around, above, beneath, and within. The God who is breath and who *gives us* breath.

What does this God who, in Tillich's words, *is* "Being" itself, require of us? Require? Can One who is non-contingent require *anything* from we who stumble forth filling our eyes, and ears, and lungs as best we can with the breath and beauty of creation? I am tempted to give Micah's reply, "*To do justice, and to love mercy, and to walk humbly with your God.*" Amen to that! My hope, however, in sharing some of my spiritual journey was to remind us to catch our breath (and God's breath) along the way. Simply put, I think God requires *more* breathing room.

I am slowly learning to give God more room to breathe. It's not always easy. At times, I find myself measuring the immeasurable. I squeeze God into my little mind and then reduce the *Ineffable* to a more containable size, causing my ideas of God to become my God. God is beyond my feeble definitions and needs more room to breathe. In other words, familiarity with the holy renders the holy, unholy. When this happens in my life the Spirit is unable to breathe fully; it slowly suffocates in the stale air of viewpoints hardened by myopic perceptions. I need to "let the Spirit breathe."

Breath, Unbidden

I would be remiss if, in these pages of prayers and reflections, I have unduly suggested that God's breath in our lives comes as a result of our bidding. Yes, we do need to take time to *talk with self and talk with God*, be it with pen in hand, song of praise, uttered prayer, or sacred silence—not as a work to be done, but as grace received. God always takes the loving initiative. God wants to breathe *on* us, *in* us, and *through* us—to wake us from lives made dull and gray by the ashes of discontent and plastic pursuits. James White put it this way, "Bread and circuses, occupy. . . our waking hours" (*New Forms of Worship*, Abingdon, p. 44). We need to discipline ourselves to step out of our frenetic lifestyle and breathe in deeply creation's blessings. However, it must be the discipline of an "unemployed worker"—one who works at *not working* to apprehend the Divine. God does not come to us because we "pray hard." God seeks to apprehend *us*; God's breath comes *unbidden*.

It *is* the breath of the Spirit that comes *unbidden* that anchors my faith. From time to time I experience what I can only call "wake-up calls"—brief unplanned and unstructured interludes of grace. How? When? Where? Why? I don't know. They *come and go as they will*: a walk on the beach, a poignant scene in a film, a painting, a dance, a turn of a phrase in a book, a violin solo—any and all of the above. Perhaps it is because I do not know the "why" and the "how" that these "breathing lessons" serve to secure my faith.

These are serendipitous moments when the *Presence* breaks in, *breathes on me*, and *takes my breath away*. Suddenly philosophy and theology vanish. All my lofty perceptions and mental constructs are stripped away, and for one brief shining moment, I have a lively awareness of an inexpressible essence of divine love and that *this* and *this* alone is ultimately *all* that really matters. All credos, programs, and formulas fade in this moment of pervasive enlightenment that is at once cognitively and emotively transfixed. It is an "aha," an irrefutable acquisition of what is intuitively known, yet seldom fully appropriated—that at the very core of creation, *everything* comes down to *love*. The Spirit, like the wind, breathes where it wills.

Where It Wills. . .

Wind. I have seen amber-gold wheat dancing in the sun, whipped by summer winds on the flat prairies of Saskatchewan. I have seen homes devastated, villages flattened, mighty oaks uprooted, steel girders twisted by howling hurricane force. I have seen whirling, swirling, ink-black clouds silence the stars and hurl their torrential tears on parched cracked soil.

Wind. I have seen sails filled, seas calmed, gentle waves, and mirrored ponds where life abounds and insects float on wispy wings. I have seen children laughing and kites flapping, soaring on winds of joy. I have seen a soft summer breeze cool a hot August night. I have seen a child's paper plane soar for miles on currents of imagination.

Wind. God's breath blowing where it will—ever stirring—ever bringing winds of change.

Wind—
Coming from nowhere, going where it wills.
Shutters slamming. Windows rattling.
Cacophony suddenly sliced mute.
Scissors of silence stilling the storm.
Air absent. Life on hold.
Aching. Awaiting.
One pale breath to stir creation's sleep.

Wind—Gentle. Kind. Refreshing.
Coming from nowhere, going where it wills.
Soft salt air kissing lips
    on seashore's gentle breeze.
Seagulls' soaring wings
    aloft on heaven's holy breath.
Newborn wrapped in love's embrace
    —a baby's breath on mother's cheek
One pale breath to stir creation's sleep.

Wind—Sweet breath of God . . .
    coming from nowhere, going where it wills,
    moving, shifting, shaping, changing,
    winging words of hope and healing,
    above, beneath, around, within.
One pale breath to stir creation's sleep.
"Let the Spirit breathe!"

Notes

1. E. H. Peterson, *The Message: New Testament with Psalms and Proverbs* (Colorado Springs, Colorado: NavPress, 1995).
2. M. Easton, *Easton's Bible Dictionary* (Oak Harbor, Washington: Logos Research Systems, 1996; original copyright 1897).
3. "Come, Holy Spirit, Come," words and music by Vicky Vaughan, copyright 1998; as found in *Sing a New Song* (Independence, Missouri: Herald House, 1999), no. 6.
4. John Shelby Spong, *Here I Stand: My Struggle for a Christianity of Integrity, Love, and Equality* (San Francisco: HarperCollins), 191.
5. Hymn text by Joseph Smith III; tune by Norman W. Smith; as found in *Hymns of the Saints* (Independence, Missouri: Herald House, 1981), no. 482.
6. Joseph Campbell, *The Power of Myth, with Bill Moyers*, ed. Betty Sue Flowers (New York: Doubleday, 1988), 3.
7. Parker J. Palmer, "The Monastic Way to Church Renewal," Desert Call, Winter 1987, 9.
8. Henri J. M. Nouwen, *The Way of the Heart: Desert Spirituality and Contemporary Ministry* (New York: Ballantine, 1985), 57.
9. Ibid., 33.
10. Henri J. M, Nouwen, *Reaching Out: The Three Movements of the Spiritual Life* (New York: Doubleday, 1975), 74.
11. Ibid., 28.
12. Ibid., 87.
13. Ibid., 88.
14. Palmer, 10.
15. Nouwen, *The Way of the Heart*, 53.
16. Anthony Bloom, *Beginning to Pray* (New York: Paulist Press, 1970), 55.
17. Ibid., 45.
18. Ibid, 65.
19. Palmer, 8.
20. Bloom, 76.
21. Ibid., 100.
22. Ibid., 26.

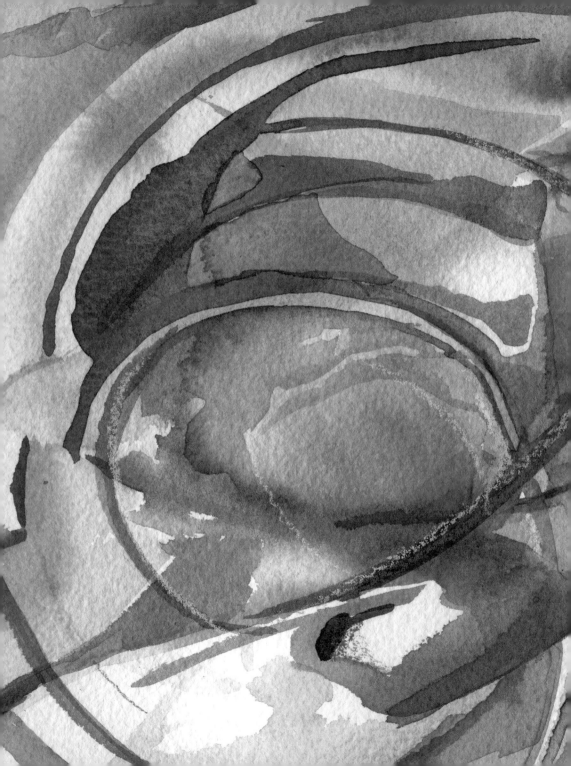